MEMORY RIDERS

An Octogenarian Bike Trip
Memorializing Past Classmates

by C. Lee Jones

To the memories of former classmates and professors who have passed away.

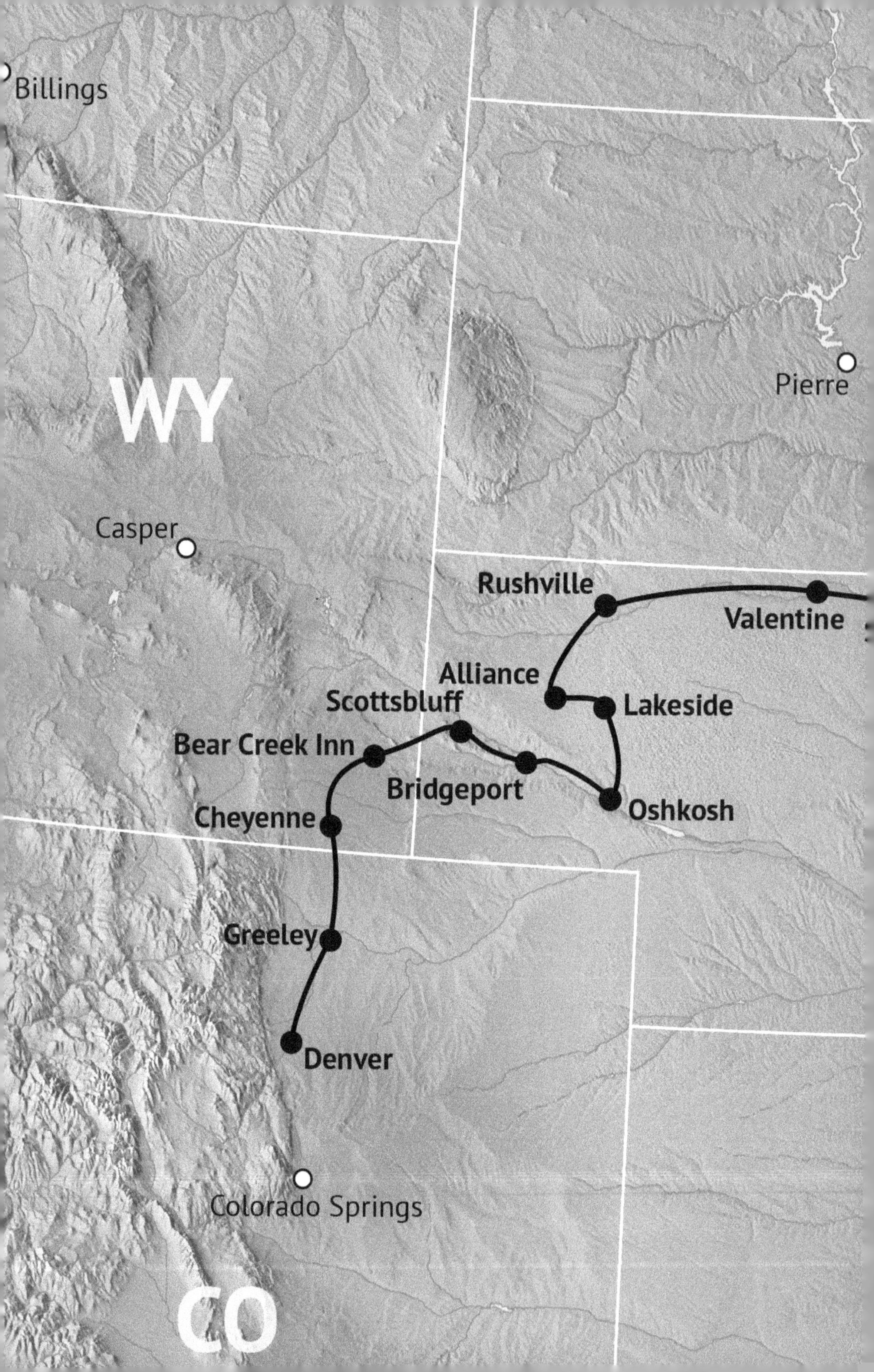
Billings
WY
Casper
Pierre
Rushville
Valentine
Alliance
Scottsbluff
Lakeside
Bear Creek Inn
Bridgeport
Oshkosh
Cheyenne
Greeley
Denver
Colorado Springs
CO

MN

Minneapolis ○○ St. Paul

Le Sueur

Lamberton

Northfield

Pipestone

New Ulm

Sioux Falls ○

Canton

te

Niobrara   Yankton

IA

Des Moines ○

Omaha ○

E

Topeka ○   Kansas City ○

Map by: One Stop Map - onestopmap.com

FOREWORD

The idea of a bike ride to my Carleton College reunion came from the desire to do a long touring trip. Naturally I wanted company, and with some recruiting on my part, the Memory Riders group came into being. One of the key attractions was the expectation of good conversation, fellowship, and sharing of experiences with trusted friends. For me, this was a sound reason to peddle all those miles. Classmates Roscoe Hill, Paul Johnson, and Lee Jones provided that element of camaraderie.

About the time I took over as the '58 class agent in 2008, I recruited Lee to start a periodic letter to encourage class solidarity. Over the years, he has presided over the highly successful *Schiller's List*. In that role, I became aware of his organizational skills and ability to get projects done superbly. As we interacted more frequently, he was a natural pick to partner with me on a long bike trip to our class reunion. Even with his limited time for training and pesky problems with his hands, he stayed committed and became a great biking companion. Once on the road with Lee, I was astonished by his deep knowledge of the wildlife, the Great Plains terrain, and American history in general. He made it a priority at every stop to accurately document his impressions and catalog our photos.

Memory Riders could not have come about without contributions from all involved. It was no less a personage than Roscoe Hill who coined the concept of "Memory Riders." His notion of remembering deceased classmates quickly gained traction. Paul Johnson stepped up to give generous support and welcome "pep talks" when we needed them. Lee deserves heaps of credit for his extensive logistics support, spreadsheets, and the use of his vehicle. In addition, he was the driving force in organizing our class ride-for-dollars campaign. His daily reports soon became very popular with more donors signing up along the way. Ultimately, this resulted in a gift of $12,500 to the College Annual Fund.

Writing a bike journal with a high level of documentation and accuracy is a daunting job. I am pleased that Lee turned out to be a first-class raconteur with a distinctive and captivating style beyond his ability to write well. This book is clearly written from the heart, which makes for appealing reading. The Memory Riders are indebted to Lee for this impressive record of our ride from Denver to Northfield, Minnesota for our 60th Carleton class reunion.

Bill Solberg -- August 2018

Roscoe Hill

C. Lee Jones

Paul Johnson

Bill Solberg

BACKGROUND

The Carleton College class of '58 has been particularly active and energized since the planning for the 50th Reunion began in the 2005-2008 timeframe. Some would attribute that energy to Whitey Nicholson, Connie Harris, Bill Solberg and a host of others involved in the planning and it persisted through planning sessions for the 55th and 60th reunions.

Early in the planning for the 60th reunion, our prolific idea generator Maisie Goodale Crowther, suggested that we encourage attendance via a variety of modes - car, plane, bus, even via bike! For reasons unknown, "bike" resonated with at least two of the committee members, Crowther and Solberg. Maisie began producing images of cyclists with scarves flying in the breeze as a proposed reunion logo and the notion was accepted. Bill, on the other hand, hauled out one of his classic bikes from many years earlier, a time when he had toured and raced with his bikes.

But staring at his bike was a long way from making a commitment to ride to reunion. While it would be possible to do solo, it would be a lot more enjoyable to have company on such a ride. The second issue before he could engage others in the project was from whence would the ride begin. It would be a stretch to get others to sign on for a ride from his home in Los Angeles to Northfield MN. (Google Maps for bike routing purposes indicates a distance of 2,028 miles.) Maybe the best way to select a starting point would be to see which classmates could be persuaded to participate. And so the search began.

Bill talked to many colleagues about his idea. I know that I was first approached in late Spring of 2017. I was not eager for such an experience but I did say that I would do what I could in a support role, like driving the SAG wagon (Support and Guidance vehicle). Bill did persuade Roscoe Hill to commit to the project and so Denver, Roscoe's home, became the starting point, approximately a thousand miles from our ultimate destination.

Bill did not give up on me and I heard from him with some regularity through the summer and early Fall. My spouse was not initially supportive of my involvement but with what appeared to be more folks involved she finally threw her support behind my participation. In early November, I told Bill that I would offer vehicular support if that was what was needed. He encouraged me to be more proactive and to actually commit to riding a bike from Denver to Northfield. So, on November 13, 2017, I bought a Specialized hybrid touring bike, called a Sirrus. I was in. Shortly afterward, Paul Johnson indicated an interest in joining our happy crew so we were now a team of four octogenarians led by our eldest member, Bill at 82, the rest of us youngsters at 81. The project looked even more possible though still intimidating to some extent.

What credits did each of us have to justify even thinking about biking something over 1,000 miles? Paul Johnson had participated in a variety of lengthy trips from hiking to sailing and upon his retirement at age 50, embarked upon some relatively serious summer biking in the Wisconsin countryside and some metropolitan trails. His biking was limited to 25 to 30 miles a day. Unfortunately, having committed to the project in December, winter was well established. Citing some personal and medical issues that required attention, Paul let us know that he was still very much interested in what we were preparing to do, but he was not going to have time to get into riding shape. Still, he wanted to help in some way. Ultimately, he ended up driving the SAG wagon the first three days of the trip and the last three days. Three riders would have to do.

Once committed to ride from Denver to the reunion, Roscoe bought a bike and began to train for the rigors of long distance cycling. He was not a stranger to bikes and riding having experience with a variety of multi-geared bikes over the years. A little more than a year earlier, he had walked across the state of Missouri on a pilgrimage led by a woman who does pilgrimages with great frequency. That experience clearly demonstrated that Roscoe had the determination to successfully complete a thousand mile bike ride.

Roscoe is known to have the capacity to assist people going through difficult personal health, life and death issues. Early in his training, in rapid sequence, three serious health issues involving close friends and relatives arose and Roscoe felt obligated to assist in each case. The timing when his presence might be required was unknowable. It meant that Roscoe could not realistically continue preparing for the ride.

Despite these distractions, he continued to help plan the trip and provided an initial headquarters for the rest of the crew before departing on our odyssey. He arranged all of the logistics for our smooth departure from Denver. We missed Roscoe throughout the trip but were delighted to see him when we did arrive on campus. Two riders would have to carry the flag for the class of '58's 60th Reunion.

Before we get to the riding pro of the group, let me share my own riding/physical exercise history. From age ten to fifteen, I rode a single speed, fat tire Schwinn newspaper delivery bike every day that I could ride. Since this was near Chicago, there were a lot of winter days when a sled or wagon was the preferred delivery vehicle. I did ride some at Carleton but strictly recreational. Not until I moved to Galveston TX did I ride seriously again, along the eleven mile seawall. That provided my exercise routine when I could not sail. The discovery of early hypertension in New York City led me to a life of running five days a week for more than thirty years, including one period where three out of four Saturdays I ran a half marathon. Exercise has been a habit for many years including using a Pilates trainer once a week for the last several years.

Faced with rusty riding chops, my early reluctance only made good sense. But, as soon as I bought the road bike, I hired a personal trainer who works with cyclists, and Yoga students among others. The key was the trainer's requirement that I report each Monday via email about the preceding week's training and what difficulties I may have had. For me it worked wonders.

But all was not roses and honey. In the midst of the training regimen, my son had to undergo three major brain surgeries for which I had to be in attendance and, hence, lost a lot of training time. In the end, he came out just fine but I fell way behind in training for a thousand mile ride. Early on I had looked at an electric pedal assist bike called the FLASH v1. Its major limitation was that it had a nominal range per charge of not more than 50 miles but we were planning average days of 55 miles. However, since we were going to have a SAG wagon, I would not be stranded if I ran out of power. So I bought one and it made my abbreviated training a non-issue.

The FLASH v1

The FLASH is a beefy (49 pounds) step through bicycle equipped with an electric motor on the rear axle supplied with power from a battery housed in the rear slanting support structure. The system has four different power settings each demanding more battery support as the selected setting is increased from one to four. The control is on the left side of the handle bars. There is a small screen at the top of the support structure which indicates the current power level and the amount of power remaining in the battery. On the right of the handle bar is the control for a normal seven step gearing system. Braking is provided by a normal mechanical disc system. The bike has a fore and aft lighting system that flashes whenever the bike is powered up. That system also includes turn and braking signals. I opted for fenders for which I was eternally thankful during rides in the rain and a basket to hold drink cages since there is no obvious place to mount them more routinely. The basket was also used to carry the battery for the iPhone X, energy foods and rain gear. While I would have loved to have the ability to have a second battery to extend my range, after the ride I felt like I had selected the right machine for the trip.

Bill's biking experience was more robust than any of the other members of the crew. He started his biking during World War II on a used fat tire, single speed Schwinn that his Dad found in a garage. New bikes were not available during the war. He recalls biking through snow drifts on school days in Minnesota. In the early 70's Bill raced in California on a Belgian steel bike and toured in England and Denmark. Bike riding became the victim of a heavy work load at UCLA. After retirement, he turned to serious sailing. In early 2017, resolved that his sailing days were over, he returned with enthusiasm to cycling. He ended up buying a high tech carbon bike with electronic shifting, disc brakes and carbon wheels. Bill also found a trainer in preparation for serious long distance touring.

Last year, after a visit to the Co-Motion bike factory, he commissioned a chromoly steel bike built to his specifications, including accommodating a short right femur bone. Outfitted with fenders, panniers, and special kick stand, he was ready to go. Before

Bill's Brand New Co-Motion Bike Ready for SAG-free Touring

setting out on the Memory Rider journey, he had ridden the new bike 4,000 miles. In combination with his carbon bike, he paid careful attention to every aspect of his kit; including properly fitted, high end cycling shoes and comfortable clothing. All of which resulted in no aches or pains from the serious mileage he had accumulated. Clearly, Bill Solberg was far better prepared than any of the rest of us for the 1,076 mile journey we were about to undertake. And, just to underscore just how fit he was for the trek, he started his ride from Douglas AZ on the Mexican border, a thousand miles from Denver!

Once the core of the team was on board, it became obvious that we needed to have a name for the project. In addition to the riding/planning team, we asked Maisie Goodale Crowther, an imaginative member of the class, to help find a name that would help describe what we intended with the project. Some of the names suggested would not have resonated in polite society. Noting that we were all octogenarians could lead you to several such monikers. "Old farts on wheels!" was one receiving some attention. Even looking back through the dozens of emails we exchanged, I could not find who finally came up with MEMORY RIDERS. But, we all felt it fit the purpose of our project and for those not immediately involved, might encourage questions that would allow us to explain in detail. Throughout the trip, the name seemed to resonate with lots of people and certainly generated questions.

TRIP STRUCTURE

With our team in place, it was time to think seriously about the elements that would assure a successful adventure. What route made sense for a cycling trip? How far should we plan to go each day? Should we consider the terrain in planning the route? Would it be possible to engage Carleton people along the way? Should we use motels, camp or a combination? How do we take care of ourselves on a three week cycling trip? What would our fallback strategies be if we met with difficulties like serious injury, bike failure, or surprise weather events? Could we expect to ride every day or should we prepare for rest days along the way? Even more critical, how far should we expect to ride between rest/rehydration/feeding stops? We knew we had a SAG driver for the first three days. Could we recruit others to drive the remaining SAG days, preferably members of the class of '58? How should we record our progress? Could we find a Carleton student who might want to produce a video to record our efforts? More important, would anyone be interested in our progress? Would daily emails or Facebook do the trick? How much and what kind of clothing will we need to deal with heat, rain and cold? What sort of bike repair gear would we need?

All of a sudden there were a lot more issues to be resolved than merely would we like to ride from Denver to Northfield! This was not a Sunday ride to the Coffee Shop. As a fundamental principle, we agreed that we would be responsible for our own costs and would share the basic common costs such as shared food, fuel, and accommodations.

Obviously, the route to follow was the major issue to be resolved. Cycling organizations provide assistance with bike routes for any number of starting points and destinations. But, almost all of them include a variety of road surfaces, trails and tracks, some hard to find. Traditional paved bike routes do not run from Colorado to Minnesota. We decided to stick to paved roads and trails since we would be riding bikes with different capabilities in terms of handling different road surfaces. Of course, the very first day out we ran into a piece of trail construction that challenged us a bit, rough gravel with ruts, and this convinced us that we would have to deal with whatever road/trail conditions we encountered. Fortunately, such challenges proved surmountable.

Roscoe Hill and Bill Solberg Selecting the Route

Just as we were searching for a routing tool, we became aware that Google had just brought out a tool for defining cycling routes on their map application. Several advisors warned us of roads/trails indicated on Google could turn out to be non-existent. But, the Google satellite feature on their map application, turned out to be an excellent way to look and see what sort of road surface we would experience as we went from one numbered road to another. The frustrating thing, speaking of road numbers, turned out to be the frequency with which a road number changed or was abandoned in favor of a road name. Even more annoying was a road number we were following going two ways at an intersection. At one such intersection, I flipped a coin and I was wrong. The one I chose lead me onto an Interstate. Time for a U-turn before Bill got led astray as well.

Our initial route selection had us going northeast out of Denver toward the northeast corner of Colorado, then angling slightly more northerly to the northern tier of Nebraska counties, then east and across a corner of southeast South Dakota and the northwest corner of Iowa into Minnesota. Then nearly straight east to Northfield. We stuck with this routing for several weeks as we tackled the next issue - motels or a combination of motels and camping.

Then how far did we want to ride each day? More importantly for those of us not named Bill, how far could we reasonably ride each day. We decided that something between 50 and 60 miles each day would be reasonable. We also listened to Bill when he suggested that rest days would make the trip more enjoyable. With rest days and an average of 55 miles per day, the ride would take from 22 to 23 days depending on the route finally selected. As we started to look at motel availability, it became clear that the route we had originally selected would either require some really long days or some camping. The problem areas were northeast Colorado and central Nebraska where motel options were much further apart than we wanted to ride each day. We started looking at alternatives to long days or camping.

Surprisingly, the best route turned out to leave Denver and head north through Greeley to Cheyenne WY. From Cheyenne we would angle north and east into western Nebraska. More than twenty years ago, my family and I discovered in this area a 50+ mile one lane road from Oshkosh NE to Lakeside NE that enchanted us so much we called it our "special road." During the eclipse event in August 2017, one of our team, Roscoe Hill, had traveled to this very road to witness the eclipse. The road crosses the heart of the sandhills, complete with lakes, miles of ranch land and loaded with a huge inventory of birds and other wildlife. By this point in the planning we knew that Bill and I were going to have to share riding/driving responsibilities in this area, so I convinced him that adding the "special road" would add a few miles but the experience would be worth it. (As I write this, my daughter visiting from Scotland, is traversing the "special road".) For those who followed our journey on a map, this part of the trip seemed to be out of the way and while it was not a direct link to our objective, I don't think either Bill or I would have traded it for any other day of the journey.

From the "special road" via Alliance NE the route went directly north to the northern tier of Nebraska counties, then east to Yankton SD, the southeast corner of South Dakota and northwest corner of Iowa and into Minnesota. It did not occur to us that the availability of motels and other places to stay in this area could be traced directly to the railroad line that had opened up this part of Nebraska. The main rail lines served the northern tier and the southern tier of Nebraska counties but did little to directly serve the central parts of the state hence we found fewer travel amenities in central Nebraska.

Arranging accommodations for the trip was an education in itself. The motels associated with chains were routine and easy to arrange and only one of these required payment in advance. Once we got into the heartlands of America, beginning in LaGrange WY, we started to meet and deal with absolutely fabulous people.

Bear Creek Inn B&B

The website used to search for a motel in LaGrange WY indicated that a B&B was just down the street from the main road. "Just down the street" turned out to be 20 miles west, the last two of which were gravel. But, the Bear Creek Inn B&B accommodation was terrific; a complete house in the ranch yard that had belonged to the original ranch owners and converted by the family into a bed and breakfast facility. Great people. Terrific breakfasts. It was a perfect choice for a Rest Day.

Then there was Springview NE that offered a house for a very reasonable rate. We received a code prior to our arrival to open the front door of a small house painted a bright green. It was as fully furnished as any high-end chain motel I have ever been in. Most of the trip planning was done via email and the occasional phone call.

It did not take long to resolve some of the safety issues we could identify. Aside from being responsible for our own daily costs, we would also be responsible for any health or personal bike related issues that might arise, though we clearly would help each other in the event of unexpected circumstances. When the team was reduced to two, it was clear that any circumstance that kept one from participating meant that the other would have to decide whether or not to proceed. Fortunately, we experienced none of these problems.

We needed to have a plan in place for severe adverse weather extending for a prolonged period. We decided to hold in place until it was reasonable to proceed. It was also decided to continue riding in light rain, but to pause if it became a heavy downpour. We experienced all of these circumstances and it was helpful to have already made decisions that fit the event.

Hydration and sufficient food were both necessary for each day to be successful. Hydration was the most critical of the two and so we decided to pause every 45 to 60 minutes and to drink and, when necessary, have a snack. We learned that a stop of more than ten minutes could adversely affect the power in our legs. One could get it back, but not easily.

We talked very little about the gear that we would need on the trip. So each of us took a slightly different approach. Since I was providing the SAG wagon, I knew we had plenty of room and paid very little attention to the space my gear took up. Consequently, I had several riding outfits so I would not have to do laundry but once a week. Bill, on the other hand, used panniers on his bike to hold everything he was going to need for the trip from Douglas AZ to Northfield. Each evening, if you were sharing a room with Bill, you had better get your immediate needs attended to quickly, because his first task was to wash out his riding gear each and every evening.

Shortly before we were all ready to gather in Denver, Paul suggested to Bill that we all be warned that in this late spring season, we should be ready for a final winter storm. That meant we each packed additional winter gear.

As for spare bike gear to take along, both Bill and I consulted our bike mechanics about what would likely be required given our unique bikes and the distances to be covered. Both of us were prepared for multiple flat tires and tools for small adjustments that might be required after experiencing rough roads. The advice was sound and proved useful.

The importance of a SAG (Support and Guidance) van driver cannot be overstated. It would have been ideal if we had had a designated driver for each and every day of the trip. We would have preferred to have classmates step up and volunteer for a few days, but, aside from Paul who was intrigued by the project from the very beginning, we attracted a few people who wished they had the time but schedules did not seem to work with the dates we had selected. Admittedly, we started trying to recruit a driver very late in the game, so we have to accept most of the blame for the lack of a SAG driver in the middle portions of the trip.

Paul Johnson, SAG Driver Extraodinaire

The SAG driver ideally makes sure that accommodations are secured for each evening, that supplies are maintained, including ice for the cooler, and that the day's route is clear and critical turns identified for the riders. When the working team is reduced to two, one drives the SAG and the other rides his bike. In this circumstance the driver goes ahead for two or three miles and awaits the arrival of the rider. Failure of the rider to appear in a timely manner sends the driver back to see what might be amiss, if anything - crash, flat tire, etc.

We all felt an obligation to record our progress but exactly how to do so was not at all clear. It was late in the planning when we tried to resolve how best to record our progress. One of the better ideas was to find a Carleton student who might need a project for an arts class who could accompany us and do the recording. Who would pay the student and how much? Unanswered, we proceeded to try to find such a student but were not successful. This was another instance of starting the planning too late.

So who would be interested in the idea of a group of octogenarians cycling from Denver to Northfield? When the question was broached, Paul Johnson was certain that what we were going to do would catch the fancy of a great many people. Would Facebook be an appropriate venue for our reports? Possibly, but we would still need to inform our classmates of daily events and progress. We did have access to email addresses for the large majority of the class but there did not seem to be any way to inform those without such access. So we decided to produce periodic emails as we went along.

In a couple of the preliminary emails to the class seeking volunteers to be SAG drivers, we included our projected route and invited any classmates along the way to let us know and we would be happy to greet them. Sarah and Carr Trumbull contacted us since our route passed just south of their home in Scottsbluff NE. A stop in Scottsbluff would not add that many miles to our itinerary and it would be a chance to visit with a classmate and her family. Sarah kindly offered to not only feed us a home cooked meal or two but to also put us up for a night. It turned out to be a highlight of the trip since we got to talk with members of the family some of whom were active cyclists with excellent suggestions for our onward journey.

In our various emails to the class, it became clear that a number of classmates were interested in the MEMORY RIDERS project. We needed a way to involve classmates in the journey without actually committing to leave their families for three weeks. We decided to offer sponsorships based on a pledge of from $.01 to as much as one chose to offer per mile ridden, assuming a minimum ride of 1,000 miles. The sponsorships would be paid to the '58 Alumni Fund and none of the funds would go toward the costs of the venture. All who sponsored the trip would get a daily report of progress. Some of the team were skeptical that such a strategy would work but we all agreed that our goal should be $10,000 added to the Class of '58 Alumni Fund. As it turned out, we were still short of our sponsorship goal when we left Denver.

Servicing the Bikes - Springview NE

Roscoe Hill, Our Denver Host

Roscoe and Paul Ready to Send Us Off

The MEMORY RIDERS Odyssey

Day -1
Gathering in Denver
Monday, May 21, 2018

Roscoe Hill, and his impeccable ability to host team members arriving at various times from various places was the focus of the days before the great adventure was to begin. I drove the SAG wagon, now with signs reading MEMORY RIDERS - Carleton College - Class of 1958 on each rear side window and the rear window. My FLASH ebike mounted on a new bike rack rode steadily from Mission KS to Denver aided by Roscoe's excellent directions. Roscoe had already had an opportunity to practice his hosting skills since he had picked Bill up in Limon CO five days earlier. Bill reported that he got a superb introduction to the central Denver area. Paul Johnson had arrived at the Denver airport a day or two earlier and had visited with his son in Greeley. His son brought him down to Denver for the initial face-to-face planning meeting of the Memory Riders.

We let everyone in the class with access to email know that we were riding in honor and memory of all deceased classmates, faculty and staff from our days at Carleton. Of our classmates who had died, five would be honored each day of the journey. As noted, those who made a sponsorship pledge would get a daily report of progress and events. As it turned out, there were a good many people who heard of our trip and wanted to be included in the daily emails. So, we had two separate lists; one for those who were sponsors of the trip and one for those who simply had an interest in what we were doing.

After completing our initial plan for the departure from Denver the next morning, Roscoe took us to a very pleasant Italian restaurant, Marcella's. It was so good that we actually pushed back our departure time a bit to make sure we all had a good night's sleep.

Day 1
Denver to Greeley

Tuesday, May 22, 2018

Our ride this day honored Bruce Anderson, Ross Bailey, Wayne Bergstrom, Herbert Binswanger, and Adele Johnson Birnbaum.

Bill Solberg and Lee Jones Ready to Start

One cannot embark upon such an adventure without a good breakfast and Roscoe made sure we had an opportunity to enjoy the breakfast of our choice at the 20th Street Cafe. A brief ride to a local park that provided access to a paved bike trail, brought the whole crew together for nearly the last time until we arrived on campus. Roscoe, Paul, Bill and I took the required initial pictures and with Roscoe and Paul shooting videos of our actual departure, we were off! The trail followed the Platte River through the city and out about ten miles where we met Paul and Roscoe. We bid Roscoe goodbye and thanks as he returned to obligations in the city. We had already encountered two sections of construction on the trail, one requiring our first gravel experience for about half a mile. No problems.

South Platte River Trail Out of Denver

Paul now assumed his role as SAG driver for the next three days. It was a learning experience for all of us. Ideally, part of his role was to make sure we followed the route agreed upon. But, the route was as new to Paul as it was to us and hard for him to anticipate each turn. We encountered road construction and had to wait to be cleared around a paving crew and that gave Paul a bit of time to get the route more clearly defined in the onboard GPS. Once cleared around the construction, we followed several back roads with little traffic until we turned onto the main highway to Greeley. Fortunately the road was wide and had generous shoulders to ride on. The truck traffic was heavy and while Bill had experienced that sort of traffic it was my first on a bike. Turned out fine and my heart rate finally returned to normal.

We arrived at our motel in Greeley, the Clarion Motel, around mid-afternoon after a relatively easy 59 mile ride for Bill and 45.8 miles for me on the FLASH ebike. The FLASH bike's reputed maximum range is 50 miles so we planned for the SAG vehicle to remain behind me near the end of the day. When I no longer had supplemental pedal power, we put the FLASH on the bike rack to finish the day.

Our motel was in the heart of downtown Greeley, a city that seemed like a relatively lively place for a Tuesday evening. We had a wonderful meal at an upscale restaurant within easy walking distance of the motel, the Greeley Chophouse. Bill was pleased that they made a good martini. As it turned out, the quality of Bill's martini would be a critical element in evaluating the quality of the evening meal.

Day 2
Greeley to Cheyenne

Wednesday, May 23, 2018

Our ride this day honored Nancy Blossom, David Boaz,
Joy Baumgartner Botts, Kenneth Brandt,
and Penelope Crawford Breitlow.

We had the first of many mediocre to poor breakfasts, though the rooms were large and well appointed. The usual pre-launch meeting was held to agree on the day's route which was pretty much straight north on the highway we used at the end of the preceding day.

Mild breezes and mostly clear skies marked the morning ride. Especially early, the sun caught the snow covered Rockies to the West and made them stand out brilliantly. To the East, by contrast, were long rolling plains of ranch land. Pronghorn antelope, some quite close to the fence underscored the fact that we were truly in the West. Many newborn calves were obvious in the herds of cattle on both sides of the highway.

I was riding behind Bill partially to be able to follow his lead in managing the heavily traveled highway. It turned out to be not much of a problem despite heavy truck traffic. We had become used to trucks giving us a bit more room and then going on by. We could hear them coming so we were ready for the pass. But, for a period we heard a truck gear down right behind us but he did not pass. I glanced back and saw that it was a rig carrying a very wide piece of road construction equipment and he needed the room on the shoulder in order to stay in his lane. We found a place to pull off the road and let him proceed. He never once honked or showed any impatience with us.

We had asked Paul to stop someplace along the way and get some ice for the cooler. The result taught us a valuable lesson. When it came time for lunch neither Bill nor I could find Paul. Places to eat were few and far between for cyclists and so we decided we had to take advantage of a place that appeared at a T-crossing. Still no Paul and no obvious place to park our bikes. We stopped for lunch but did not feel sorry for Paul since he had the entire inventory of food we had in the SAG wagon. Efforts to communicate with Paul were not productive until well after lunch. To avoid repeating this confusion, we agreed to shop before we started the day or after we finished.

As we approached Cheyenne WY, huge, beautiful thunderheads developed in the northwest but we experienced no rain.

A Rest Stop with Rockies in the Background

Entering the Bear Creek Ranch Area

We arrived at our motel at mid-afternoon after missing just one turn. The ride for Bill was 53 miles and for me on the FLASH 49.7 miles before I ran out of battery power. None of us had ever been to an Outback Steakhouse so we had supper with them. I had hoped for better quality but it was at least OK. No martini risk this evening.

Day 3
Cheyenne to Bear Creek Inn

Thursday, May 24, 2018

Our ride this day honored William Paisley Brown, Robert Buell, Lindsay Cooper Calhoun, Jon Candy, and Sheldon Carlson.

Motel office "coffee" (a misnomer if ever there was one) sent us off to a nearby cafe for breakfast. But, the day was absolutely gorgeous; clear blue skies with light winds to start. Many pronghorn grazing or napping on the rolling countryside, always alert and curious. The terrain began to change slightly as we neared the eastern edge of Wyoming. Bluff features marked creek drainages and interrupted the rolling hill environment. Bird song everywhere - meadowlarks, grass sparrows, western kingbirds, and many more not identified.

At around mid-day, the wind began to pick up and for a long while was a strong tailwind. Then our route turned almost due north and the wind became a strong sidewind necessitating strong pedaling action even when going down hill.

We arrived at Bear Creek Inn on the Scheer Circle Triangle Ranch, our destination for the next two days, early in the afternoon. Bill had ridden 59.5 miles (not the last two gravel road miles) and I had ridden 51.9 miles on the FLASH. It was the first day over 50 miles for the ebike.

Paul had served as our SAG driver for the first three days, but his son was going to pick him up in Cheyenne this evening. So, we piled into the SAG and drove back to Cheyenne, had dinner at a western style saloon, dropped Paul off and returned to the Bear Creek Inn. We traveled the Cheyenne to ranch route three times this day but it was worth it each and every time. Beautiful country that changes with each passing hour and cloud formation.

When discussing making accommodtion arrangements above, I did mention the fact that the B&B at the ranch was a complete house with plenty of bedrooms and baths for a party of several more than Bill and I represented. The kitchen was stocked with everything one might need. Despite the remote location of the ranch, internet service was available if you knew where to sit.

Day 4: Bear Creek Inn

Friday, May 25, 2018

This was a Rest Day for us and we could not have picked a better place for a rest day, comfortable beds, great showers, and all the breakfast you could wish for. Not only this, but our hosts, the Scheers, were a delight as well. Husband, wife and son work the 5,000 acre ranch and their daughter, whom we did not get a chance to meet, works the neighboring 8,000 acre ranch.

When we got up in the morning, we went over to the ranch house and were invited in to breakfast with the family. They were wonderful hosts provided good coffee, several juice flavors, thick French toast and wonderful sausage. Then more coffee and lots of informative discussion about ranch operations.

After breakfast we cleaned and serviced our bikes, did some laundry and then set out to see what LaGrange WY was like. It is a very small town but did have a consolidated school and evidence of lots of school activities. Since it was about lunchtime we decided to try the only cafe/grocery in town, the Longhorn Grocery & Cafe. This was one of those jewels you occasionally stumble upon in the sparsely populated American West. Operated by folks who'd been running it

for more than forty years, they obviously were committed to delicious food. There were very few folks inside when we entered but shortly after we ordered, the place filled up with folks who clearly were local workers. They knew the drill for the menu of the day and the owners knew what their customers wanted. Bill and I both ordered BLT's and were treated to home-baked bread, crisp bacon and fresh lettuce and tomato. Neither of us had had a better BLT anywhere. We were bold enough to try the cherry pie and were once again well rewarded. Should either of us pass this way again, we will certainly be there for lunch.

We spent the afternoon exploring Hawk Springs Recreation Area. It is located a couple of miles off the main north/south highway but in country as apparently empty as this, we were surprised to encounter a crowded camp and recreation area. Lots of folks fishing and kids enjoying what kids enjoy around water. We had thought we might do some bird watching but had a hard time finding a place to park and suspected that the afternoon here was not the best bird watching time. Early and late would have been better. We did not realize it at the time, but the crowd was certainly a reflection of the Memorial Day weekend just beginning.

Sunset - Bear Creek Inn

Our B&B hosts had indicated that there were two places for supper in Hawk Springs, the Long Branch Grill or The Emporium, just a few miles north, but that we would probably be happier with The Emporium. It turned out to be something less than what its name would suggest but the steak was decent and the owners engaging. Bill likes a martini before his evening meal and he had learned how to make one in a special way on his journey from the Mexican border to Denver. The Emporium was one of several places where Bill was allowed to provide detailed instruction on the construction of this special martini. Evidently they were good students.

On the way back to the ranch, we again spotted mule deer and turkeys. A beautiful sunset reflected off of surrounding bluffs made for a memorable evening drive.

Day 5
Bear Creek Inn to Scottsbluff

Saturday, May 26, 2018

Our ride this day honored Robert Christensen, Fred Cooper, Sandra Stillman Cors, Lawrence Cox, and Edward Dahlin.

Today was the first day that Bill and I had to share SAG driver responsibilities while the other one rode a bike half the distance to our objective for the day. I was fortunate enough to ride first, and while we skipped the gravel portion of the road out, we started the ride as soon as we reached blacktop headed East. As one might expect when traveling out of a canyon, one enjoys a downhill ride. It was a glorious morning again and I was enjoying the ride, the countryside, the birdsong, when suddenly I realized that a large creature was moving along the roadside on my right. It was a large mule deer and she was intent on crossing the road ahead of this man-machine on the roadway. She finally put on a burst of speed and dashed immediately in front of me. Fortunately, my bike has an excellent set of brakes or I might have been wearing that mule deer. She was a beautiful creature though.

The deer sighting was followed a couple of miles further on by turkeys moving through a fence into the high grass beyond. Because the first part of my ride was mostly downhill, I covered 19.6 miles in the first hour. Just as I reached the halfway point of our ride, our route turned due North toward Scottsbluff NE and our hosts for the night Sarah and Carr Trumbull. Sarah was a classmate of ours at Carleton and when she discovered we were traveling relatively close to Scottsbluff, she invited us to overnight with them and we accepted. The added miles were insignificant when compared to the prospect of a home cooked meal.

While the first leg of our travel to Scottsbluff had been mostly downhill, when Bill took over the riding, he was faced with a seriously long uphill slog with temperatures creeping into the 90's. I waited for him at the top of the range of hills we were

*Only with Excellent Eyesight
Can You Spot the Deer*

*Carr Trumbull
- Sarah Skinner Trumbull's Husband*

traversing and was greeted by a couple of cyclists who knew the Trumbulls. They had simply ridden out from town to the hilltop to enjoy the long downhill ride back home. Bill arrived just in time to greet them and share some experiences as cyclists seem to do whenever they meet.

As the SAG driver, I was responsible for making sure we turned at appropriate points to get to our destination. I missed a turn so GPS came to the rescue and we arrived mid-afternoon to a warm reception. The Trumbull's even made their garage available for us so we could recharge the FLASH bike and the SAG wagon which is a Ford C-Max Energi which uses battery power to supplement gasoline fuels. It was the only time on the trip when we could recharge the SAG, but it was welcomed.

Once the vehicles were cared for, we were provided with showers followed by a welcoming beer. Several of the Trumbull youngsters, some with families of their own, stopped by to talk with us. Privately, I thought for awhile that they might show up just to see what a couple of octogenarians attempting a thousand mile ride might look like. It was nothing like that at all. They were as genuinely interested in us as people as we were of them. Supper was lasagna, salad and more dessert than I could have wished for.

A good night's rest followed by a huge breakfast and we were just about to set off when a son of the Trumbull's who was a cyclist showed up to talk with us. He gave us some timely tips on exiting Scottsbluff and we headed for the days objective, Bridgeport NE. Frankly, we hated to leave the Trumbulls. They were terrific hosts and we did not come close to exhausting all the tales we wanted to hear from them, nor the tales we wanted to bore them with. We looked forward to seeing them a couple of weeks hence at the Reunion. (Apologies to Sarah, whose picture I failed to get.)

Day 6
Scottsbluff to Bridgeport

Sunday, May 27, 2018

*Our ride this day honored David Deleo, Virginia Delfs,
Charles DeLong, Rebecca Robinson Denny,
and Clifford Dimmitt.*

With great local knowledge guiding us out of Scottsbluff, we made terrific time toward our day's destination, Bridgeport NE on little traveled roads with wide shoulders. Our route took us past several cemeteries that were already decorated for Memorial Day. We enjoyed tailwinds all day long though we traveled only 40 miles or so. Tailwinds helped shorten an already short day. My FLASH and I averaged nearly 22 mph though I had ridden almost as quickly as I could. We rode through flat ranching country with very few hills to worry our progress. The rain has been so prolific in this country that the irrigation equipment has yet to be put into operation, but it is a green landscape with herd after herd of cattle.

Because it was such a short day, in the afternoon we took the time to visit the Pioneer Trails Museum, a local museum of regional history. The founder of the museum gave us a detailed, personalized tour of the place. It was interrupted only with the arrival of another group of visitors. Clearly there is a great deal of local pride in this community and many are willing to share items from their past for display in the museum. It also underscored the time periods that both Bill and I have lived through. There were lots of things that I recalled from the late '30s and '40s, toys, old telephone system components. Remember the party line and your two short and one long ring, at least that was ours on the farm in the '40s?

Our motel was the Meadowlark Inn & Restaurant with a heavy emphasis on liquor store. The room was easily large enough to accommodate our two bikes. The food would keep you alive but not encourage a return trip though breakfast the following day was at least average.

The forecast indicated that we should expect heavy rain over night. The SAG will appreciate it since we have accumulated a layer of dust over the entire vehicle. We may even face some rain on tomorrow, day #7.

Day 7
Bridgeport to Oshkosh

Monday, May 28, 2018

*Our ride this day honored David Doty, David Drake,
Patricia Eliet, Tucky McCarthy Elliott, and Frank Ewing.*

The forecast was accurate. Thunder and lightning punctuated the night along with torrential downpours. For a bit after we awoke it was crystal clear, punctuated with clouds on the horizon. We stayed dry on the way to breakfast but had to dodge showers to get back to the room. Fortunately, we could see more bright skies to the West and the weather was moving East. By the time we were ready to depart, the rain had stopped and it looked like it might be a decent day to ride.

It was my turn to ride first and I was blessed with mild headwinds that did not hold me up much. But when it came time for Bill to ride the wind picked up, stayed as a head wind and made his ride much more difficult. Our route paralleled a pair of railroad tracks and we were treated to one train after another. Trains loaded with coal going East and empty coal cars going West. In this country ranches had their own private railroad crossings and they were so marked.

Fortunately, our route did not require us to cross those tracks until very close to our day's destination.

Throughout our adventure we saw three other long range riders, each riding alone. Bill would invariably stop and exchange news and destinations with them.

Our destination was Oshkosh NE (not WI). It was Memorial Day and when we arrived we discovered that the cafes were all closed. The only place to get supper was at the 24 hour, all-purpose gas station. We were just about resigned to visit the gas station for supper when the motel owner came by to tell us that the ELKS club in town was having a burger fry at their facility and that everyone was invited. Saved by the ELKS. They prepared burgers to our specifications, had plenty of fries and a variety of beer options. It was a fine supper, especially when faced with the alternative.

Bill on the Way to Oshkosh

Day 8
Oshkosh to Alliance
(via Lakeside)

Tuesday, May 29, 2018

Our ride this day honored Joanne Johnson Ewing, Sarah Johnson Foley, William Ford, Jr., David Garwood, and James Gladish.

Once again, a strong storm passed over our motel during the night, leaving limbs down in the parking lot. There was no damage to vehicles that we saw. The morning started with broken clouds and a forecast that suggested the possibility of scattered thunderstorms. We left too early for the cafe to be open so we resorted to the all purpose gas station for ice and a breakfast snack. We did carry a food box with plenty to keep us going so this was not a hardship, rather a choice.

This is the day we planned to travel the "special road" described in the early part of the narrative. From Oshkosh the road heads straight North as a two lane blacktop for two or three miles and then transitions into a two lane, well maintained gravel road. Three or four more miles and the road becomes a single lane, sandy gravel road since it is crossing the sandhills of West central Nebraska. Bill was riding the first segment and had no difficulty on the blacktop or the first few miles of gravel. But, as the proportion of sand to gravel grew the impact of the rain from the preceding night made the surface very soft. Bill's road bike tires sliced right through the sandy gravel bringing his progress to a halt.

We unloaded my FLASH bike and secured Bill's bike on the SAG bike rack. Just as we were about to set off, we noticed a beautiful tortoise making its way off the road into the sandy hill country. A little larger than an adult's hand, it had a beautiful shell and was unperturbed by our rather close examination.

The FLASH and its much wider tires handled the sandy gravel road surface just fine with a minimum of slipping and sliding. Making good progress, I was hopeful that I could get to the Crescent Lake Wildlife Refuge visitors center. Not yet. It began to rain and though I had a rain jacket on, it felt like hail was pounding my shoulders. It was not only uncomfortable, it hurt. I stopped and we loaded the FLASH for another mile or two. The rain stopped and we unloaded FLASH and I proceeded.

Lee and FLASH Skidding on Special Road

As we got closer to Crescent Lake, the terrain kept getting lower and lower. With the rain in the recent hours, water was flowing over the road in spots. I paused and evaluated one such area but I could clearly see that the water was no more than a couple of inches deep though it was several yards wide. I decide to ride through it and no matter what to keep going. I was fine until I got within six or eight feet of the other side. The bottom fell out and the water was nearly up to my hubs but I had decided to keep going and did so. Suspecting that the electric motor would short out, I kept going but with one ear cocked for any strange sounds or any pause in the power

supplementing my pedaling. No impact. FLASH just kept going and did whatever I asked it to do.

The rain returned along with its imitation of hail. We called a halt, loaded both bikes and decided to drive to the end of the "special road." I drove this segment to the paved highway and before we got out of the National Wildlife area, Bill took a couple of short videos. One was of a herd of cattle on the road several members of which were reluctant to make way for the SAG, others kicked up their heels to get out of the way.

Horses Eager for Attention

The second one recorded us fording a section of road with water actively flowing across it. At one point the sandy brown bow wave of the SAG could be seen nearing the top of the hood.

Despite weather issues we did see cattle and horses on the road. The cattle were skittish and the horses were delighted to have their necks scratched even in the rain. Before the rain began when Bill was still on his bike we encountered pronghorn and whitetail deer. Saw no mule deer this time through the area. Despite the weather distractions, we did manage to see a white faced ibis, lots of ducks though mostly mallards, a gambrel, a golden eagle and an unidentified hawk. With wind and rain, it was hard to see many grassland birds which are usually everywhere you look.

We did take advantage of a brand new visitors center facility on our way to the paved highway. Once we got to the highway at Lakeside and the road leading back to Alliance, site of our motel for the evening, I launched again, this time into 10 to 20 mph headwinds. It did not take long for FLASH to run out of power.

We got Bill set up and underway. He too was riding into that fierce headwind. He was still making progress but it was slow. Even going downhill, he had to pedal hard to make progress. That did not last long. We loaded his bike and motored into Alliance. It had been a difficult day, but I do not think either Bill or I would trade it for any other day of our journey.

Water Over the Road

Day 9
Alliance to Rushville

Wednesday, May 30, 2018

Our ride this day honored Donald C. Green, Walter Griga,
Alice Highland Gruia, Don Harris, and Carolyn Hall Hartman.

The motel in Alliance was more modern than most of our accommodations, but left no distinguishing memories for either of us. Supper was undistinguished as well.

Morning saw us on our way a bit earlier than usual since we had a stop in mind early in the ride and a relatively long ride to boot. It was my day to start the ride and I wanted to show Carhenge to Bill, a local family's version of Stonehenge built entirely with old automobiles. Yes, it is odd but it grabs almost everyone's attention. The site is overseen by the state though it is still a private, no fee area. Recently, other auto related sculptures have been added, fortunately at a distance from the original structure. Each time I have visited, I've been greeted by a staff eager to share the history of the place and to hear your travel story as well. Ours, as was usual, generated sufficient interest to encourage another photo opportunity by our hostess.

Once back on the road, I was faced with a quartering headwind, but with pedal assist, it did not hold me up much. In fact, it was my objective to cover my portion of the day's route as quickly as possible since we were expecting some pretty warm weather

in the afternoon. After only 20 miles, FLASH ran out of power. It was my biggest FLASH disappointment of the trip. Only after the fact did I realize what had happened. In trying to cover as much territory as possible, I had alternated between pedaling very hard with fairly long coasts. It should have occurred to me earlier that whenever I started to pedal, the motor would kick in putting an initial surge on the battery and that initial surge put more drain on the battery. Coupled with a headwind and using a higher power setting, I was demanding an extraordinary effort from the battery system. My intent had been to get my part of the ride finished as quickly as possible but I had pushed the system to its limits in a very short time. Bill was forced to take over for the remaining two thirds of our route. Shortly after trading places, Bill was rewarded when our route turned more toward the East and the quartering headwind became a quartering tailwind. He had had more than his share of headwinds so this was a welcome assist for him.

In fact, aside from the lesson I learned about the power situation with my bike, it was a lovely day to ride. We were traveling

Carhenge

through the gently rolling hills of Nebraska's sandhills with lovely blue skies and puffy white clouds that increased gradually over the course of the day.

In Hay Springs we stopped at another of those all-purpose gas station/grocery/cafe/hardware stores. The hot dogs were palatable, the cokes cold and the bananas fresh. The folks running the place could not clear their one table fast enough for us. They were very hospitable. We got the feeling that they even called some neighbors to come see the cyclists in their fancy gear. One elderly gentleman drifted by as we were preparing to leave and observed that we had traveled further in our trip than he had in his life except, of course, when he was in the Army.

We arrived in Rushville, our designated stopping place only to find no one in the motel office. A gentlemen saw our predicament, greeted us saying that he was Sioux, not Blackfoot - evidently there had been some local difficulties between the two and he wanted us to know he was one of the good guys. In any case, he told us the proprietor would not be back for another few hours. We went into the very small office; found the record of our reservation and the room we were assigned and registered ourselves. The proprietor did show up that evening and thanked us for helping ourselves.

Rushville, like so many other towns along this northern tier of Nebraska counties, is smaller than it used to be. In fact, towns of more than 350 were the exception with many even smaller. Youngsters are more attracted to the larger cities and towns. So there are a lot of empty store fronts. We identified two cafes and selected one more by its size (large) than by its ambiance (missing), Yoba's Tavern. The locals were already at the bar but the booths, probably 40 feet away, were available. There were plenty of game areas available for a busier night - pool and darts seeming to be the primary entertainment. By this time, we were short on greens, so we ordered salads wherever we ate. These were forgettable but the burgers were properly prepared and the beer just OK.

Best news of the day was from Paul Johnson who let us know he would join us June 10th in Lamberton MN and be our SAG driver from there to Northfield. That means both Bill and I will be able to ride the last three days of the journey.

Day 10: Rushville

Thursday, May 31, 2018

This was a REST DAY for us, chosen because my family has some history associated with Rushville. We needed some laundry done today and I ended up driving East to Gordon NE for the nearest coin-op laundromat. It was empty, clean and everything I needed worked.

For lunch we decided we would like to find some Mexican food since we had seen an ad for a Cantina in Rushville. We were assured by Rushville's all-purpose gas station, that there wasn't such a place in this town but we could find one in Chadron NE, just 45 miles West. It was a rest day so we took off for Chadron. When we asked, we were told that there used to be a Mexican cafe right over there, Wild's Bar & Grill. Well, that's where we went hoping that there might still be some Mexican cuisine still on the menu. The meatloaf sandwiches were unique but not bad and not Mexican.

That afternoon we visited the Sheridan County Historical Museum in Rushville which has grown substantially since last I visited. My reward was finding my grandmother's picture along with other members of her PEO chapter. They also let the meaning of those initials out of the bag, formerly a very big secret.

One of the challenges during our trip was making sure we had good internet access so I could get the daily trip reports out. We were having trouble getting any sort of access in Rushville until I visited the public library. In years past, at least one of the library clerks remembered certain members of the family. During this visit, some folks who were remotely related to our family were recalled. That was interesting, but the main thing was their internet link was very strong and offered all the power I needed to get the daily report on its way.

When reservations were made for this part of the trip, our preferred motel had a room for only one of the days we needed, so we made one day reservations for each of the two motels in town. It required moving but that was not a big deal. The internet service did not improve at the second motel however. When we first arrived at the second motel, the parking area was empty and this was the one that had indicated it was full. By supper, it was completely full of oil service trucks.

For supper, we decided to go to the other cafe in town, the Twisted Turtle. The ambiance was terrific. The owners were personable and interested in everyone in the place. The pizza could have used some assistance but the beer was terrific. I'll return to this place the next time I visit.

On the way back to our motel, we discovered a very small sign on the 20 Bar saloon on the main street announcing the presence of a Cantina. We would have been better served if we had but seen that sign before setting off for Chadron.

Day 11: Rushville to Valentine

Friday, June 1, 2018

*Our ride this day honored Maria Anne Harvey,
Paul Bauer Henkel, Bruce Herrick, Nancy Klenk Hill,
and Helen Williams Holmes.*

We left Rushville relatively early since this leg of our journey was the longest one day ride we scheduled, 105 miles. Because of my abbreviated ride out of Alliance and because I thought I had the answer to extending the mileage my battery could sustain, I led off the trek. It seemed that my theory was right. I covered 50.8 miles before I had to turn the riding over to Bill. While I had not gotten my 50% of the load done, I came very close and was delighted.

During my driving period, I twice lost Bill. I had been riding with a slight quartering headwind. Shortly after Bill started his ride, the wind shifted and became a quartering tailwind. Both times when I lost him, I had driven several miles ahead and parked to await his arrival. During those waits, I often caught up with emails and thought about what I would say for the daily report to sponsors. Both times, Bill sailed past me and was almost ten miles ahead when I finally found him. The gently rolling roadway with wide shoulders and a wind assist, helped Bill to fly like the wind. I learned to pay more attention when I was driving the SAG wagon.

This day gave us some sense of just how extensive the sandhill region is. We rode all day through this beautiful countryside full of gently rolling hills, bright green fields, widely scattered trees and large herds of cattle. There were a lot of calves in each herd and all would turn tail and run away from the bike as it passed but seemed unperturbed by the vehicle, even if it stopped near them.

Valentine NE was our destination and a huge very dark cloud seemed to be stuck right over the city. Despite preparations to get wet, we stayed dry as the cloud was just East of Valentine. The one change that we welcomed was the cooler temperatures that seemed to come out to meet us as we neared our destination.

Our motel, the Raine Motel, had a large restaurant and bar so we did not have to go far for supper. As mentioned earlier, Bill had been taught how to make a particularly good martini and when he found a willing student, he was not shy about sharing his new-found skill. This young bartender learned her new skill well and Bill was more satisfied than usual with the results.

SAG Wagon Catching Up on Email

Day 12
Valentine to Springview

Saturday, June 2, 2018

Our ride this day honored Richard Hopeman, Janet Johnson, Kermit Johnson, Wendell Johnson, and Don Jugle.

When we got up and went to breakfast, it was clear that something had happened overnight. We did not know whether it was something international, national or local. We finally found that the city of Valentine had suffered a huge loss during the night. Like many towns along this northern tier of counties, the coming of the railroad helped the communities through which it passed to prosper. In Valentine, an entrepreneur with foresight built a large hotel right across the street from the train station with a saloon on the ground floor. The building had ceased being a hotel several years ago but the saloon had been turned into a restaurant, the Cedar Canyon Steakhouse. The entire structure had burned to the ground during the night. The former hotel portion of the building had been rented out to employees of the saloon. All escaped safely and were quickly accommodated by other motels in the area. We could not get to the front of the building as we left in the morning but passed by on the street just to the East. The ruins were still smoldering and hotspots were being heavily watered. The rumor mill had not yet suggested a cause of the fire when we left. (Twenty days after our departure, Valentine and the surrounding area was struck by a 3.5 magnitude earthquake.)

Valentine attracts a great many sportsmen for the great fishing and hunting in the area. So there is some hope that, at a minimum, the restaurant will be rebuilt to help meet these local demands.

Valentine sits on the eastern edge of the sandhill region. Bill was the first rider today and as soon as he got out of town, he was immediately in the rolling hills of the Niobrara National Wildlife Refuge complete with buffalo and elk. While we did not see any of them, each entrance to the refuge warned against approaching these or any other wild animals. Given the rolling nature of the road he was riding on, Bill averaged over 16 mph and on at least one occasion was traveling well in excess of 30 mph.

Staying Properly Hydrated
was a Daily Requirement

Ruins of the Cedar Canyon Steakhouse

Lee and Bill - Springview Selfie

Once Bill had ridden his half of the day's route, I got my chance at the rolling hills. But, there was just one serious descent and then things flattened out. I did enjoy a rear quartering tailwind and covered 22 miles in just an hour and ten minutes.

When we arrived in Springview NE, a community of 300 souls, we quickly found the house we had rented, the Springview Town House. The day before, the owner had texted a four digit code that would open the front door. It worked, opening into the most completely furnished and equipped accommodation of our entire trip. Painted bright green, it was equipped with everything you might wish in your own home including great wi-fi.

We had arrived just before noon and found that our only cafe option was the familiar all-purpose gas station just a block away. We ate sparingly, walked the town from one end to the other and then spent the afternoon tending to our bikes, reading and napping.

Supper we discovered on our walk could be had at the Cattlemen's Saloon that opened at 6:00 PM. We got there a bit early but were welcomed in to discover that the two folks operating the saloon were on their first days on the job. Fortunately the cook had a bit more experience. The salad was really good and the barbecue reasonable. We both had a beer not wanting to test the skills of the barkeep.

Day 13
Springview to Butte

Sunday, June 3, 2018

Our ride this day honored Douglas Keasling,
Roger Kirschner, William Knoblock,
Margaret Derosier Korsch, and Faustina Larned Lees.

This was yet another mild day with plenty of sunshine, scattered clouds and mild winds that started as a slight quartering tailwind, moved through almost 360 degrees before settling into a pleasant tailwind. The rolling ranch land continued with plenty of wildlife. Riding the first leg today, I startled two mature turkey gobblers in the bar ditch. They did not fly but ran with me down the fence line trying to find a way through that fence. Having to watch the road, I never did see them get through the fence.

Bill's ride was also punctuated with wildlife some of which he even saw! He did see a turkey hen that ran across the road in front of him and scurried into the tall grass on the other side. What he didn't see was a beautiful full-bodied whitetail doe that bounded away from the fence and across a huge pasture. I was driving just behind him at the time or the event would never have been noted.

Given that it was a Sunday, we thought we might see a bit more traffic but the traffic remained pretty normal except in the fields. Sunday or not, the ranchers were busy in the fields making hay while the sun was shining. Some fields nearly a mile long had hay raked into long rows ready for baling; other fields had balers, tractors, wagons and trucks all engaged in baling and collecting the cured hay. Then there were other fields that had just been cut and not yet raked into rows and others that had yet to be cut. It was a busy haying day everywhere we went today.

It was a short riding day and we arrived in Butte NE at our motel the Oak Creek Inn just before noon to discover we had less than an hour before the only cafe in town shut down until Tuesday morning. It seems like the owner was heavily involved in firefighting when required but his wife ran the cafe, the Firehouse Bakery & Cafe. They were, as usual in this part of the country, hospitable and eager to tell us all about their community. The BLT's were good and the drinks cold. We could only wish that they were going to be open the next morning for breakfast. But, no such luck.

Lee Headed for Butte NE

It continued to be pleasant all afternoon. Supper came from our food box and some prepackaged foods available from the motel office. We availed ourselves of a bench facing the Eastern horizon as it changed colors on the way to dark. Lots of swallows helped control the insect population and so our bench time was insect free.

Day 14
Butte to Niobrara

Monday, June 4, 2018

Our ride this day honored John Levine, Judith Frees Loredo,

William Lydecker, Brita Frost-Hansen Mack, and Marlena Mayer.

Breakfast was again a combination of our food box and selections from the motel office, selections not to be confused with culinary satisfaction.

Bill led off the bike riding this morning. The route was going to be relatively short, something under 50 miles. The breeze was out of the South and the cool early morning became comfortably warm in the mid-80's by the time we reached Niobrara NE. The early part of the day continued through ranch country busy with haying. There seemed to be a lot more cutting today than on Sunday. That may be because there are more helpers available on the weekend for the really heavy work of loading and hauling.

Our route lately has been on well maintained state roads but often without much of a shoulder to give cyclists a bit more room. We have been following NE 12 for the last few days and have one more day on this route before heading northeast into South Dakota. Shortly after I took over the bike riding, we encountered a road crew stripping away the surface layer of the road and just as quickly laying down a new surface layer. This required single lane traffic alternating each direction. Initially the traffic I was in moved slowly enough for me to keep up with no difficulty. But, once we got beyond the active working party, the speed picked up to a rate I could not hope to match. I finally found a place to move off the road and let some very pleased car and truck drivers move on at their preferred speed.

Before I cleared the construction zone, the road began its way through the hills bordering the Niobrara River. The terrain offered some interesting descents and the newly repaved road had a few additional inches of space for cyclists which is always welcome.

It wasn't long before we came to Niobrara which sits entirely on top of one of these hills, all 370 souls. Bill is sure there were more than that. Arriving early in the afternoon, we looked for a cafe for lunch but were forced to opt for another all-purpose gas station. We took the time to drive all of the streets in Niobrara and came to the conclusion that this was not where we would enjoy spending a rest day. We were scheduled to spend the next day in this village with darned little to occupy us.

No Pause Here on the way to Niobrara

Upon returning to our motel, the Hilltop Lodge Motel, I tried to send off the daily report but discovered that while the place often had wi-fi, it was not operating this day. Even the proprietor could not get on. She did suggest that I go sit on the bench in front of the public library where I could get a good signal. It was a very strong signal with no difficulty sending off some fairly large files.

While touring the village, we did discover a grocery store cum hardware store. They had not yet received their resupply yet, so the fresh fruits and vegetables looked a little tired and at the moment we had no need for any hardware. We also discovered a saloon that offered a place to have dinner. It turned out that Bill could get a reasonable martini and we both enjoyed a dinner of walleye pike and a decent salad. This place must be one of the few places open on Monday night and it was full by the time we left for a good night's rest.

Day 15
Niobrara to Yankton

Tuesday, June 5, 2018

Our ride this day honored Janet Bettinghaus McAullife,
Jean Schwolow Mohrig, Mary Kimbark Morison,
Terry Moshier, and Joan Hooker Neumann.

As noted above, Bill and I could not see ourselves taking a rest day in Niobrara. In a single afternoon we had exhausted all that the community had to offer. We might have commissioned a fishing guide for our rest day but we would still have been confined to the community afterward. We called ahead to our scheduled motel in Yankton SD, the Econo Lodge, our next stop and they were only too happy to have us arrive a day early and continue with our previously made reservation. Yankton is many times larger than Niobrara and we trusted that it would have much more to offer.

The Niobrara motel did offer coffee in the morning and a power bar but we supplemented that with some yogurt, bananas, and fruit juice. We were well fed by the time we left. I led off the bike riding this morning and loved the long descent out of Niobrara down to the flatlands along the Niobrara River.

After Bill took over, we left the Niobrara and started to move through the hills beside the Missouri River. Those hills were steep with quick descents and then another sharp climb. There seemed to be

Discovery Bridge Over Missouri River into Yankton South Dakota

Meridian Double Deck Bridge

more traffic this day but, as usual, very accommodating. I had to gear way down on one particularly steep hill, the road had no shoulder to ride off the roadway. I was still about 200 yards from the top when a large truck came up behind me, slowed to my pace until he could see over the top of the hill before passing. I appreciated his safe approach to the situation.

The bridge over the Missouri is a handsome four lane structure with large ornamental pillars all the way across. One passes from Nebraska into South Dakota at mid-bridge. As we have come to expect, our motel is always on the other side of town. Since we arrived prior to noon, we set out to find some lunch.

To our surprise, we found a street vendor with a line waiting patiently. That's always a good sign unless everyone has poor taste. They didn't. The bratwurst was excellent and the fries above average. It was a nice introduction to Yankton. We returned to our motel and serviced our bikes since it had been a while since the last good cleaning.

With the advice of the desk clerk, we set out to find a place called The Landing for supper. It turned out to be an excellent restaurant with precisely the martini required by Bill and excellent entrees and salads. Only Bill had room for dessert but it looked fantastic. They were offering special pasta dishes the following night and we decided to return.

Day 16: Yankton

Wednesday, June 6, 2018

Though a day later than scheduled, this was our REST DAY and we certainly picked the right place for it. Yankton, aside from Denver, is one of the largest cities we spent any significant amount of time in. Located along the Missouri River and served by a major railroad line, the city was a significant communication hub in its earlier days.

Initially, ferries and pontoon bridges made the link between the two states. The pontoon bridges were built twice each year; once to carry traffic over the ice and once to carry traffic when the river was ice free. River traffic is minimal now but is heavily used as a sport fishing venue. The rail service continues carrying mostly coal from what we could observe. The city made an investment in a public park along the river. It was undergoing some renovation during our visit but it looked like a wonderful place when open. The park was built around the north end of the two deck Meridian bridge originally built to link Nebraska and South Dakota and replace the ferries and pontoon bridges. The top deck was intended to carry automobile traffic and the bottom deck rail traffic. For economic reasons, the railroad never completed their portion of the project intended to move rail traffic north and south so the rail portion of the bridge was never put to use. The automobile traffic grew to the point that the lower deck was modified to carry car traffic and for several years each deck carried one way traffic for a $.50 toll each way. In 1993 the bridge was placed on the National Register of Historic Places.

Safety issues forced the construction of the new Discovery Bridge which opened in 2008. The Meridian was closed to traffic and converted to a bike and hiking trail still linking the two states and during our visit midweek had several groups taking advantage of the bridge. Having spent the morning exploring the park and bridge, we found our street vendor for another helping of bratwurst and fries.

We had seen a very tall church spire on the west side of Yankton and decided to explore that area more closely. It turned out to be a hospital, college, monastery and large chapel. The college is Mount Marty College; the monastery is Sacred Heart Monastery (Benedictine); the chapel is Bishop Marty Memorial Chapel and the hospital is Avera Sacred Heart Hospital.

We had noticed earlier in the day that there was a 3-D Star Wars film showing so we headed that way. We were treated to what amounted to a private showing since we saw no other people in the audience. We both enjoyed *Solo: A Star Wars Story*. By the time it was finished, it was time to return to The Landing and another really fine meal.

Day 17
Yankton to Canton

Thursday, June 7, 2018

Our ride this day honored Jon Nicholson, Richard Nuzum, Karl Thomas Opem, David Patten, and James Porter.

We awoke to a soft but steady rain and a forecast that indicated it was going to be wet most of the day. This was one of the longer days, 70 miles, so it tested our grit for dealing with rain. Bill had thought this out pretty carefully and had brought a complete set of rain gear from helmet cover to cycling shoe covers. He kitted up and looked as though he dared any water to get through.

However, by the end of his half of the ride, he was almost as wet inside his gear as he might have been riding in the rain without the protection. It wasn't the heat since we started at 62 degrees and only barely got into the 70's by the end of the ride in Canton. But, his gear just did not have enough ventilation to get rid of his own generous internal heat.

Bill had the first ride on this day and faced mild headwinds until we finally turned North toward Canton. After the turn North, we got some modestly assistive sidewinds but picked up a lot more traffic. They had closed a US highway for construction and had re-routed that traffic onto our state road. But, as usual, drivers were courteous and gave us plenty of room to ride safely.

When driving the SAG wagon, the usual practice is to go ahead for a few miles, find a place to pull off the road and await the arrival of the rider. Following that routine, I had found an apparently little used gravel cross road and parked so I could see across the road as well as both ways on our road. It was not unusual for me to spend some time looking for birds and other fauna at these stops. Across the road and down a slight slope, I noticed some tall grass moving in a way contrary to the mild wind and kept an eye on the area. I was rewarded when three fully mature turkey gobblers crossed the road. The largest of the three stopped as though posing for all to admire and strutted in full display as he finished crossing the road. They were really beautiful birds.

*The Norwegian Roots of the Area
Are Still Evident*

Bill in His Rain Gear

By the time it was my turn to ride, the rain had slacked off to occasional drizzles and my light rain jacket was all I needed. But with the winds and the rain, during which we tended to ride a bit slower, it was still a 6 3/4 hour day. Our pauses may have been a bit longer in hopes that the weather would pass us by.

Once again, when we entered Canton, we found our motel, the Gateway Motel, on the far side of town. Why is it they never build our motels on the near side?

It turned out that the two-bed room was one of the smallest we had on the entire trip. We could barely get our bikes inside with room to move around. But, we found a rather nice restaurant, the Black Angus Steakhouse, that had a friendly staff and fine food; one of those places you would gladly return to if offered the chance.

Day 18
Canton to Pipestone

Friday, June 8, 2018

Our ride this day honored Robert Priest, Nelson Prins, Peter Prins, Arthur Radtke, and Donald Rail.

We were greeted in the morning with a bright sky to the East - our route initially this day. A bit of pseudo coffee from the motel office and some breakfast from the food box and I was ready to head off into that bright sky which it turned out I had ignored after the first few minutes of the day. One of the folks who keeps the motel in good shape came out and asked to take our picture. The word had gotten out of our venture and I think she wanted some evidence of these octogenarian travelers.

As I took off for the first ride of the day, Bill went after some ice for the cooler. He noticed some very dark clouds to the West and North of town. For my part, as I exited the town limits, I finally realized that the bright sky had become awfully grey and was tending toward black. Cars now had their lights on. Bill was not close so I made a plan for getting caught in really bad weather. I would get off the bike, put my rain jacket on and huddle down under my own arms if no other cover was available. Aside from hard rain, I fully expected hail from such a black cloud. I kept going and it kept getting blacker. Then there was Bill going by and the clouds began to brighten with nary

a single drop of moisture being deposited on my route. I felt like I had escaped one that time.

Our route crossed into the very Northwest corner of Iowa. But, in Larchwood IA, I missed the fact that the road we wanted went straight and the larger highway curved Northwest before proceeding North and back into South Dakota. Neither Bill nor I understood what had happened but we were clearly on the wrong road and it was a very rough road with almost no shoulder for cyclists. Suddenly, my front fender came loose. It did not fall off but I needed to tend to the situation immediately. It turned out to be a relatively easy fix that held for the remainder of our odyssey. The stop gave us a chance to consult Google maps and figure out where we had gone wrong. There were two options; take a chance on what appeared to be a shortcut or, bite the bullet and take the long way across to the route we wanted to head North to Pipestone. This was one of the only times we disagreed but I was riding and I did not cherish taking another chance so I opted to go straight East to the road we were looking for. I paid for my stubbornness by dealing with three miles of

Bill at Full Throttle

the strongest headwinds I encountered on the entire trip. But, it worked. To give Bill credit, his route would probably have saved us a couple of miles and kept me from having to deal with wind right on my nose. My only reward was a couple of miles of strong tailwind once we got on the proper route. However, now it was time for Bill to ride.

With the favorable wind, Bill was flying. So I drove several miles past him and parked to await his arrival. I had once again selected a gravel cross road. On the other side of the highway the road went gently down a long hill to some railroad tracks where a train was parked. As I waited for Bill, two vehicles drove down to the tracks and parked to await the movement of the train. As I waited, two cock pheasants moved from a planted field on the right to a pasture on the left. They were in no hurry, apparently knowing full well that it was not hunting season. When I finally left the site, the train was still standing and the vehicles were still waiting.

Despite weather and directional problems with Bill's fast pace we were in Pipestone by early afternoon. Our motel, America's Best Value Inn, was not all that far from where we entered town for a change but the road around it was under re-construction and it was a mess. The entry to the motel parking area changed from one hour to the next as the construction proceeded.

We serviced our bikes and got a little rest before setting out to find a place to eat. We found a brand new steakhouse that had just opened, the Stonehouse Supper Club. Everyone was new but there was an effort to work out efficient systems. The steaks were excellent along with the salad. It made for a great night's sleep.

View of the Morning Sky When Getting Ice in Canton

Day 19: Pipestone

Saturday, June 9, 2018

We had delayed our previous REST DAY for one day, and we had another scheduled for Pipestone. Since all the remaining accommodations had already been arranged, we opted to take the final REST DAY as scheduled. At this point, we were just 12 miles short of 900 miles of riding.

We both wandered around in t-shirts and shorts but I discovered that I must have pretty thin blood since the on and off rain and cool temperatures forced me to pull out a long sleeved t-shirt by mid-afternoon.

We visited the Pipestone County Museum where Native American influences on the community were evidenced in nearly every exhibit. Two other influences impacted the community as well, multiple fires and three railroads. Three fires took out schools and resulted in larger and improved replacements. Other significant fires included a dry cleaning establishment that involved an exploding fuel tank, the complete destruction of a very large and imposing hotel, and an oil tanker fire that destroyed several oil storage facilities as well as oil cars on the railroad. There were two fatalities in the oil tanker fire.

The rail developments were all initiated near the end of the nineteenth century. One lasted no more than a couple of years. The other two had longer histories; one serving the north-south traffic and one the east-west traffic. Both were ultimately acquired by larger rail companies and by 1960, the last passenger train service was halted.

We then stopped at a private pipestone and Native American artifact store, Keeper's Gift Shop & Gallery. It was located in one of the former rail passenger stations that had been moved to the present site. While its mission to teach the art of making stone pipes was announced by a very large replica outside, the most commanding feature on the grounds was a huge sculpture of a draft animal, probably a mule.

At lunch we discovered a combination bakery/cafe, about half devoted to each mission, Lange's Cafe. It was packed and after eating their fare, it was obvious why. Would that we had found it for this morning's breakfast. Our departure tomorrow is scheduled to be too early for the place unfortunately.

We had carved out the afternoon to spend at the Pipestone National Monument. A detailed and well done film was an excellent introduction to the history of the place and the art involved in creating the Native American pipes. This is not the only such quarry in the US but it is by far the largest and served most of the Western tribes.

The Visitor Center included several Native American artists making a variety of pipes and artifacts. One gentlemen saved all of the dust from cutting the stone, mixed it with resin and poured it into a variety of molds. A touch or two of paint results in decorative pins and earrings.

There is a trail into the quarry but the rain picked up just as we were ready to set out. I suspect that each of us will return to take that trail at some time in the future.

We had looked unsuccessfully for a Mexican cafe while in Rushville NE. We found one here in Pipestone, Los Tulipanes Mexican, and enjoyed a really fine version of Mexican cuisine and beer.

Mule Statue, Pipestone MN

Day 20
Pipestone to Lamberton

Sunday, June 10, 2018

*Our ride this day honored Nancy Bell Reierson,
Michael Resnick, Barbara McElroy Rezny,
Melvin Roblee, and Donna Peterson Rock.*

Both of us are energized today since we will be meeting Paul in Lamberton at the end of our ride. Will be great to see him and welcome him back to our happy band of travelers.

Starting out a poor-to-bad omen is discovering you have a flat tire. Bill's front tire was flat despite the time we had taken to service our bikes during our rest day. He was prepared and we got the inner tube replaced and the tire properly inflated. Now the day could start.

We were alerted to the fact that there was a paved bike trail that extended for many miles following an old railroad bed that parallels the highway we were going to take anyway. Bill had the first ride and I went along to make sure we could find the beginning of the trail. We found it and Bill was off in a cloud of dust (figuratively speaking).

Driving back to the motel and highway we were to follow today, I found I was passing the bakery/cafe and thought I might just stop in and get a chocolate doughnut or something. With mouth awater, I pulled in, found a parking spot, got out and reached for my wallet. Gone.

Just what I needed. Returned to the motel and searched the room and my baggage twice. Nothing. Drove back to the Mexican cafe and there was a clean-up crew that let me in and helped me look. Nothing. By this time, I had given the car a once over on two occasions. Nothing. I was beginning to wonder if Bill had accidentally put it in his gear when I got a call from Bill.

The paved trail had given out and become a very bumpy track. He was simply letting me know that our rendezvous point was no longer valid and that he was just now getting back onto the highway.

"Where is That #@*& Wallet?"*

Paul Rejoins the Crew in Lamberton, MN

I shared my wallet loss with Bill and he reassured me he did not have it and we noodled other alternatives. Finally, I decided to get several miles ahead of Bill and take everything out of the car. By this time we had stuff stored all over the place in the vehicle. I pulled over next to a beautiful lake, Wilson Lake. Bill had agreed to stop and help search the car when he got up to me. My first move was to open the back door behind the driver's seat and remove the cooler. There was the wallet right under the driver's seat. Whew.

With the lost now found, I had some time to watch the lake and the birds in the area. Saw a pair of pelicans seemingly trying to teach three smaller ones to handle the wind. It was windy, giving Bill his usual challenge. The adult pair would make a nice gliding turn into the wind and the smaller ones would try to emulate the move. While I watched they went from tumbling nearly backward

when impacted by the changed wind direction to actually making decent turns and adjusting their flight. Also saw a bald eagle being harassed by several much smaller birds.

It was my turn to ride and I dealt with headwinds for a couple of miles and then with a turn in the road actually got a bit of a helping quartering wind. This is about when we passed through Walnut Grove MN, home of Laura Ingalls Wilder. This is also when a light rain began to fall just as the road turned again and I was facing a headwind. Every single pedal stroke was assisted by the battery, even when going downhill and at 28 miles, 6 miles short of my assigned part of the ride, the FLASH gave out. (Several weeks later, I discovered that if I had simply put the bike in the granny gear, I could have managed as much as 10 miles an hour pedaling and finished the ride.) But, Bill took over just as Paul showed up and helped everything look a lot better. Paul had beaten us to the motel, the Lamberton Motel, and had the beer cold and ready.

Paul had asked a friend to drive him out to Lamberton from St. Paul and then return his car and pick him up in Northfield three days later. What a wonderful friend to have given that the weather was not particularly inviting for a trip of more than 160 miles.

Since it was Sunday night, the only place to get a bite to eat was the local saloon, Lj's on Main. The exterior was not particularly inviting but the proprietor was welcoming and happy to sell us some microwave pizza or should I say a slab of cheese. The beer was good though and the popcorn free.

Bill Demonstrates That There is More Than One Way to Get Soaked

Day 21
Lamberton to New Ulm

Monday, June 11, 2018

Our ride this day honored Edwin Rossow, Sydnie Vowles Simpson, David Smith, Susan Dreyer Southwick, and Robert Stanley.

Some cyclists enjoy riding in the rain but Bill and I had experienced rain for almost the entire time since crossing the state line into Minnesota. We awoke this day to a soft, steady rain. Not what we had been hoping for. After breakfast the rain seemed to have relented and the weather radar looked as though we might get out from under the rain clouds. We left, today accompanied by Paul, who took over driving chores for the final push to Northfield. That meant that both Bill and I could ride. It was nice to be riding together again.

Though the rain had turned to a soft mist, at least temporarily, the temperature fell into the 50's. But, as we pulled into Springfield MN the rain returned with a vengeance. We pulled off the highway and took shelter under the portico of a drive-in bank facility, SouthPoint Financial Credit Union. Since it now appeared that the rain was here to stay for awhile, Bill pulled on his rain gear - again covering himself from head to toe.

The rain did ease off a bit and we decided to ride straight through town rather than take the highway which clearly circled the north edge of town. Unfortunately, we took a wrong turn and rode a couple of miles in the wrong direction before we tumbled to our error. The day's ride was right at the best range of FLASH, so this error led to my failure to make it to our destination before battery power was exhausted.

The temperature had not warmed verymuch and I was really cold and almost happy to lose power and require a lift the last several miles. It would be the last time on the journey that I would need such a lift.

Our stopping place for the evening was New Ulm MN and true to form, our motel, Microtel Inn & Suites, was on the far side of town. Bill found this pattern unusual, but consistent with the pattern he had noticed on his Mexican border to Denver route. I reviewed the strategy I had used for selecting our motels and could find no pattern that would lead to such a result.

Lunch was a pleasant affair at a nearby Applebee's. Bill's brother had alerted him to

Bill Under Way
in Full Rain Gear

Artifacts From the
Minnesota Music Hall of Fame

the presence of the Minnesota Music Hall of Fame and we had spotted it on the way through town. After Bill called to see if they could get a tour despite the fact that the place was not open on Monday, Bill and Paul set off to explore the museum while I tried to compose the day's travel report.

The museum, devoted mostly to "old time" German bands and their instruments, started its Hall of Fame in 1989 and Doc Evans was in the first group of inductees. Other notables whom I recognized included Bob Dylan and Judy Garland (1991), St. Olaf Choir (2013), Garrison Keillor (2016) and John Denver (2017). Both Paul and Bill remember a good many of the polka bands that are included. The engaging curator who gave the tour of the museum even pulled out her concertina and played a tune for them.

Paul had lived in the area years ago and recommended Veigel's Kaiserhoff German restaurant for supper. Paul had frequented the restaurant nearly fifty years ago when he had been politically active. At that time it had been the top German restaurant in the area. It still looked and felt like a German restaurant but sadly it also looked like it had seen much better days. The food was really good and the beer exceptional. We all hoped that the place would survive with some reasonable modernization.

Day 22
New Ulm to Le Sueur

Tuesday, June 12, 2018

Our ride this day honored Robert Stewart, Patricia Affeldt Stout, Lowell Stoutland, Mary Logan Trischett, and Joan Marsh Turner.

We've been on the road now for three weeks and for Bill, counting his trip from the Mexican border to Denver, six weeks. I frankly thought that long before this, I would be showing signs and feeling signs of being tired. But neither Bill nor I have shown such signs. We attribute this to a schedule that included appropriate rest days, daily rides that left time to recharge at the end of each day and great strategy and initial support from Roscoe Hill and driver support the first three and last

Lee and Bill Headed for Le Sueur MN

three days of the trip from Paul Johnson.

We have not yet seen the sun during our initial days in Minnesota and rain has been plentiful. Fields have standing water and the streams are bank full including the Minnesota River. Some flooding has been reported though we have not encountered any since the sandhills of Nebraska. Today the weather report suggested that we might escape rain and so we did until the last minute or two as we pulled into the Value Stay Inn parking lot in Le Sueur when a very light mist fell for a few minutes.

We rode on good roads as we had come to expect in Minnesota. We made a turn though onto the roughest road we had traveled on so far and it had no shoulder either. It lasted only seven or eight miles when another turn put us on a fine Minnesota county road with a bit of a tailwind to boot.

For those interested in the perceived performance problems of the FLASH ebike, it was at about this point that I think I realized the root causes of those problems. First, I had not been checking my tire pressures each morning. When I did check the pressure yesterday, I was a third down from normal resulting in increased rolling resistance and so requiring more effort on both my pedaling and the battery. We also speculated that low temperatures and headwinds may have contributed to fewer miles per charge. On the Lamberton to New Ulm ride, I tried to stay behind Bill so we could stay closer together regardless of terrain. That meant that I would pedal a revolution or two and then coast but as soon as I started another pedal cycle, the battery would take a bit of a surge in demand to start sending the required power to the motor. This extra load on the battery each time the motor kicked in would likely reduce the mileage available per charge. That is exactly what happened when I tried to stay behind Bill. I could see the power bar indicator lose a bar more quickly than I was used to. On the New Ulm to Le Sueur ride, I tried to pedal continuously no matter whether I had to pass Bill or he passed me. With this constant pedaling strategy, I covered 44 miles and still had two power bars out of seven remaining. Subsequently, I have tested this theory several times and the results have been consistent. Steady pedaling with modest power settings and modest gearing demands results in much more mileage. Using slightly elevated gearing and varying power settings results in lower mileage by as much as 40%.

Paul had lived and worked in Le Sueur for several years and knew the town well. He took Bill on a driving tour while I got the daily travel report out. In fact, Paul says he got his professional start in Le Sueur where Green Giant was king. He and Bill had lunch at the country club and found it to be a mere shadow of its former self, much like the town. However, when it came time to find a place for supper, we had a difficult time. We finally found a Mexican restaurant, Chabilitas, where we once again found good Mexican cuisine but this time the beer was only average.

Day 23
Le Sueur to Carleton

Wednesday, June 13, 2018

Our ride this day honored Marilyn Arko Umehara, Deborah Hankel Van Stone, R. J. Van Stone, Maria Ebert Warner, Paul White, John Wightman, and Ann Von Komaromy Woodhouse. Thus, at the end of this day we had ridden to honor the memory of all 97 classmates who died before us. We hope their families have felt a major part of the 60th Reunion.

When Bill first thought of this bike ride, I feel certain that he envisioned our arrival on campus on a bright, sunny day. Our weather record in Minnesota did nothing to suggest that we might actually enjoy such an arrival. But, lo and behold, we left Le Sueur under glorious blue skies and sunshine and they persisted for the entire ride to campus.

Our ride continued through rolling hills in typical Minnesota farm country dotted with lakes. I paused a couple of times just to take in the lovely lake scenery, each complimented with an obligatory heron or two. Our route was relatively short and wind was no factor at all. It almost felt leisurely.

The roads were excellent, especially in Rice county. They rolled gently and curved gently with an occasional burst of rip-roaring downhill to give us a bit of a thrill. Rather than being able to see miles down the road, the curving nature of the road meant all of a sudden finding ourselves in the middle of a great small town like St. Thomas MN and its gorgeous church. Paul thought he remembered a classmate from St. Thomas, possibly our classmate Janet Shaughnessy whose son had been a close friend of Paul's son.

Our route took us through Montgomery MN and Paul alerted us to the fact that the community was well known for its kolacky rolls. Unfortunately, we were about a month too early to enjoy the towns celebration as the world center for kolackys complete with a prune spitting contest. But, to make sure we did

Beautiful lakes and streams

Montgomery MN's Kolacky

not miss out on this world-class Eastern European delicacy, Paul drove into town and picked up some samples. Looking a bit like a dinner roll, stuffed with a variety of fillings and topped with a bit of frosting, they were nothing like anything I had ever had. I tried to compare them with boyhood memories of kolache, but the comparison was pretty weak. (Seeking Google guidance, I discovered a range of Eastern European baked goods including Kolachi, Kolache, Kolacky, Kolaczki, Kolachky, and Kiffles.) There seems to be room for another five world centers for the remaining delicacies.

We had been in contact with the college about our arrival and alerted them to our plan to have lunch in Dundas, or thereabouts. We were subsequently contacted by Carleton Professor Lutsky a cyclist who suggested that we stop in Millersburg for lunch at an establishment called Boonies and he would meet us there.

There was also the prospect that some other cyclists would join us at that point. We arrived before Boonies opened at 11 AM but seeing customers lounging around outside, they opened immediately and made us all feel welcome. We took advantage of their open air patio and enjoyed a BLT and a coke.

The professor showed up and we enjoyed talking local cycling with him. Just as we were about to depart Boonies, four more cyclists showed up to escort us into

Paul talking with Carleton Professor of Psychology, Neil Lutsky, Who Had Ridden Out to Millersburg to Greet US

Arriving on Campus to a Wonderful Greeting

Maggie Patrick with Lee and Bill. Maggie was a Wonderful Source of Support for the MEMORY RIDERS

Northfield via a paved bike trail from Dundas to Northfield. The cycling group around Northfield must be pretty close since in addition to the cyclists with a connection to Carleton, there was a townie who had heard of our journey and wanted to be part of welcoming us to his hometown.

Once in the town center, it was clear that we were early for our announced arrival time on campus. We lounged around a bit, thanking our escorts for their efforts and their obvious enthusiasm for the journey we were about to complete. A few minutes after 1:30 PM, we rode down College Street to the entrance to the college campus and were greeted by what appeared to be almost the entire Alumni Affairs Office, complete with banners,

cheers and hugs of congratulations. Before I could even dismount, President Steve Poskanzer strode up, fresh from meetings away from campus, and warmly greeted us. He let us know that he had talked about our odyssey at his commencement address the preceding week. While it might have been more dramatic to arrive after the reunion had actually begun and classmates were on site, this welcome was more than we had expected and was an emotional end to the actual biking trek.

Awareness of our accomplishment went well beyond those greeting us upon our arrival. After we had been interviewed and photographed by the *Carleton Voice* and the *Northfield News* (we were front page news in the next issue), I went off

President Poskanzer Greeting Us on Arrival

to find a place to park the SAG wagon. Walking back to get Bill and take our bikes to a garage for safekeeping, a woman walked up to me, identified herself as a college employee and asked if she could give me a hug. She and her officemates had followed our progress via the daily reports that were posted outside one of the offices. She was thrilled with what we had accomplished and wanted to let us know it.

The following day, my wife who had-flown up to join me for the reunion, was sitting in the bus headed for the campus from the airport. She overheard someone say, "Some Dude is riding a bicycle from Denver to Reunion!" Not sure how they heard of our trip but it was indicative of the number of people during reunion who knew about the journey and wanted

to hear more about it. The students who help make every reunion actually function smoothly, seemed to all know about it and even what we looked like. We had shared photos along with our daily reports, so that was probably the source of the identification.

After all the welcoming on the day of our arrival, Bill and I were once again left to our own devices for supper. Paul had already been picked up by his friend and would return to campus later during the reunion. We walked downtown found one of the old haunts and enjoyed a heavy supper complete with my first and only martini of the trip. After a good night's sleep we had the next day to unwind and get ready for a variety of reunion activities.

Friday evening, June 15th, the classes from the 1950's were invited to a reception in the garden of the President's home. The Memory Riders, all four, Roscoe Hill, Paul Johnson, Bill Solberg and Lee Jones, had a photo opportunity with the President. It was a fitting conclusion to a marvelous experience, one we shall never forget.

The President also made certain that we each got a copy of his commencement address during which he had mentioned our odyssey. It was as follows:

> "The friendships you have gained here will also endure. For example, as I speak, Bill Solberg and Lee Jones, members of the Carleton Class of 1958 - the class that started the Schiller tradition! - are riding their bicycles across the country together to their 60th reunion next week. Bill started at the border with Mexico and Lee started in Denver. they're riding in memory of former classmates and professors who have passed away. Classmates are cheering them on through Facebook and have pledged gifts to Carleton for every mile they ride. They're a shining example of Carleton traditions of community, creativity, loyal generosity, and lifelong friends."

We thanked him for his kind words and support throughout the planning and execution of our venture.

Finally, while we did not arrive at our goal of $10,000 in sponsorships prior to our departure from Denver, we did pick up a few additional sponsors during the ride. At the reunion, some classmates were sufficiently impressed with our feat that they increased their sponsorship levels while others jumped in with additional sponsorships. Once all was settled, total sponsorships for the Memory Riders came to $12,500. The participants in the Memory Rider odyssey thank each and every member of the class who helped make the trip and the addition to the Alumni Fund such a success. That means every member of the Carleton class of 1958.

Both Bill and I have been asked many times since finishing the ride whether we would willingly do it again. The short answer is, "Yes." It would be a very different experience the next time around given what we learned. Our days would probably be longer and the overall trip shorter. It would be hard not to start from Denver though, given the wonderful support and arrangements provided by Roscoe. We would make certain to have a SAG driver for the entire trip and, if I were still riding an ebike, it would be one with changeable batteries so I could ride as much as 80 to 100 miles a day without putting a burden on my compatriots. Better yet, all riders might consider an ebike.

Finally, we would try to have both Roscoe and Paul riding with us. When might we undertake such a trip again? At our age, waiting for the 65th Reunion, doesn't make sense. Might we do something for the Mini-reunion that is being discussed? Maybe.

We'll all wait and see. In the meantime, let's all go for a ride.

Paul, Bill, President Poskanzer, Lee and Roscoe

CPSIA information can be obtained
at www.ICGtesting.com
Printed in the USA
FSHW011054021218
54174FS

9 780692 190395